REDEEMING YOUR DAYS

Take advantage of every opportunity because these are evil times.

Ephesians 5:16 *CEB*

by
Franklin N. Abazie

Redeeming Your Days
COPYRIGHT 2016 BY Franklin N Abazie
ISBN: 978-1-94513309-1

All right reserved. This book or any portion thereof may not be reproduced or used in any manner whatsoever without the express written permission of the publisher, except for the use of brief quotations in a book review. All Bible quotes are from King James Version and others as noted.

Published by: F N ABAZIE PUBLISHING HOUSE—aka, Empowerment Bookstore

That I may publish with the voice of thanksgiving and tell of all thy wondrous works.
Psalms 26:7

To order additional copies, wholesales or booking call:
the Church office (973-372-7518)
or Empowerment Bookstore Hotline (973-393-8518)

Worship address:
343 Sanford Avenue, Newark, New Jersey 07106
Administrative Head Office address:
33 Schley Street Newark New Jersey 07112
Email: pastorfranknto@yahoo.com
Website www.fnabaziehealingministries.org
Publishing House: www.fnabaziepublishinghouse.org

This book is a production of F N Abazie Publishing House. A publication Arms of Miracle of God Ministries 2016.
First Edition

CONTENTS

THE MANDATE OF THE COMMISSION......................iv
ARMS OF THE COMMISSION…………………………..…..v
INTRODUCTION..viii
CHAPTER 1
The Number of Your Days...........….........…........1
CHAPTER 2
Investing Your Time.................................15
CHAPTER 3
Maximizing Your Potentials...................................19
CHAPTER 4
Prayer of Salvation...47
CHAPTER 5
About the Author..55

THE MANDATE OF THE COMMISSION

"The moment is due to impact your world through the revival of the healing & miracle ministry of Jesus Christ of Nazareth.

"I am sending you to restore health unto thee and I will heal thee of thy wounds, said the Lord of Host."

ARMS OF THE COMMISSION

1) F N Abazie Ministries—Miracle of God Ministries (Miracle Chapel Intl)

2) F N Abazie TV Ministries: Global Television Ministry Outreach

3) F N Abazie Radio Ministries: Radio Broadcasting Outreach

4) F N Abazie Publishing House: Book Publication

5) F N Abazie Bible School: also called Word of Healing Bible School (W.O.H.B.S.)

6) F N Abazie Evangelistic Ass: Miracle of God Ministries: Global Crusade

7) Empowerment Bookstore: Book distribution

8) F N Abazie Helping Hands: Meeting the Help of the Needy Worldwide

9) F N Abazie Disaster Recovery Mission: Global Disaster Recovery

10) F N Abazie Prison Ministry: Prison Ministry For All Convicts "Second Chance"

Some of our ministry arms are awaiting the appointed time to commence.

HIS DESTINY WAS THE CROSS....

HIS PURPOSE WAS LOVE....

HIS REASON WAS YOU....

Christ hath redeemed us from the curse of the law, being made a curse for us: for it is written, Cursed is every one that hangeth on a tree:

That the blessing of Abraham might come on the Gentiles through Jesus Christ; that we might receive the promise of the Spirit through faith.
Galatians 3:13-14

INTRODUCTION

In my opinion, time is the building block of life. In God's own eye, our time is precious and the determinant factor, directly proportional to the productivity of our life. We must all understand the value of our life by investing wisely and maximizing our God- given time here on earth. A lot of us have wasted away our precious time, thereby wasted away our life. In this book, *Redeeming Your Days*, you will agree with me that time, wisely invested, is proportional to our lifetime output.

> *Redeeming the time, because the days are evil.*
> **Ephesians 5:16**

But the NIV translation puts it this way:

> *Be very careful, then, how you live—not as unwise but as wise, making the most of every opportunity, because the days are evil*
> **Ephesians 5:15-16**

A great man, Benjamin Franklin, once said, "*time is money*." This great man went forward to say, "Dost thou love life? Then do not squander time, for that's the stuff life is made of."

I have witnessed friends and most of those related to me squander their time, as if there is a spare life. Without contradiction, **"Time Is Money."** Most of us in the Western part of the world understand this principles. But the majority of us in Africa-Nigeria do not acknowledge this truth. Colossians 4:5 says, *"Walk in wisdom toward them that are without, redeeming the time."*

> *Therefore be careful how you walk,*
> *not as unwise men but as wise,*
> *making the most of your time,*
> *because the days are evil.*
> **Ephesians 5:15-16** *(NASB)*

The Greek root word for REDEEM is the word exagorazo—which has two root meanings from two Greek words: "ek" (meaning from or from out of) and "agorazo" (meaning to purchase). This word means to buy back, salvage, rescue or resuscitate.

Put another way, we are to **redeem—or buy back—our time because we live in an evil time.** The Greek word is "kairos," which means "time." But not just any idea of time: It's not about the rotation of time or a measurement of time. Rather, kairos deals with the set time—the due time or right time. We must all live our life to the fullest in our own generation—GOD-given time.

> *It is not for you to know the times or the seasons,*
> *which the Father hath put in his own power.*
> **Acts 1:6-7**

> *And there were four leprous men*
> *at the entering in of the gate: and they said*
> *one to another, Why sit we here until we die?*
> *If we say, We will enter into the city, then the famine is*
> *in the city, and we shall die there: and if we sit still here,*
> *we die also. Now therefore come, and let us fall unto the*
> *host of the Syrians: if they save us alive, we shall live;*
> *and if they kill us, we shall but die. And they rose up in*
> *the twilight, to go unto the camp of the Syrians: and*
> *when they were come to the uttermost part of the camp*
> *of Syria, behold, there was no man there.*
> **2 Kings 7:3-5**

A man once said, "If you cannot fly, run. If you cannot run, walk. If you cannot walk, crawl." We must keep doing something positive as long as we live.

What does this mean?

Our lives are built around a set time. As long as we are alive, we must be positive about the outcome of our lives. Faith must continue to inspire us to engage our hands in meaningful work. Jesus said in John 9:4, *"I must work the works of him that sent me, while it is day: the night cometh, when no man can work."*

In this life, we must not only do something positive to improve our life—we must leave a legacy for the future generation. Do not give up because you do not have a job. Do not be frustrated because you lost an employment, suffered a set back or was a victim of divorce. Do not reduce yourself to a beggar because your rich uncle promised you millions of dollars, but failed you at last. Your help is not supposed to come from your uncle, but from above. *"I will lift up mine eyes unto the hills, from whence cometh my help. My help cometh from the Lord, which made heaven and Earth."* (Psalms 121:1-2) In the race of life, taking absolute responsibility for our lives is the gateway to a greater future. A man once said, "Decisions are the horses we ride to **fame** or **shame**."

To everything there is a season,
and a time to every purpose under the heaven:
A time to be born, and a time to die; a time to plant,
and a time to pluck up that which is planted;
A time to kill, and a time to heal; a time to break down,
and a time to build up; A time to weep, and a time to
laugh; a time to mourn, and a time to dance;
A time to cast away stones, and a time
to gather stones together; a time to embrace,
and a time to refrain from embracing;
A time to get, and a time to lose; a time to keep, and a
time to cast away; A time to rend, and a time to sew; a
time to keep silence, and a time to speak;
A time to love, and a time to hate; a time of war,
and a time of peace. What profit hath he that worketh
in that wherein he laboureth
Ecclesiastes 3:1-9

Happy reading!

HIGHLIGHTS
HOW TO REDEEM YOUR DAYS

REPENT

*And the times of this ignorance God winked at;
but now commandeth all men every where to repent.*
Acts 17:30

For a long time, we have lived in **sin** simply because of ignorance. *"And the times of this ignorance God winked at; but now commandeth all men everywhere to repent."* Our first step to **redeem** our time is to **repent and surrender** our life to JESUS CHRIST. *"Casting all your care upon him; for he careth for you."* (1 Peter 5:7)

Until we are willing to **repent of our sins,** God is not **willing and ready** to **"restore our lives."** **Repentance** is the gateway to a greater future. Peter replied to a question from the crowd "what shall we do?" with: *"Repent and be baptized every one of you, in the name of Jesus Christ for the forgiveness of your sins. And you will receive the gift of the Holy Spirit."* (Acts 2:38) Every time you truly **repent**, you are on a step ahead to redeem your time.

FAITH

*For as the body without the spirit is dead,
so faith without works is dead also.*
James 2:26

In **this race of life**, our plans and heart desires cannot be accomplished unless there is **faith inside of our heart**. FAITH is so POWERFUL that it is an anchor of HOPE. FAITH is the lifeline upon which we must build our lives. *"He staggered not at the promise of God through unbelief; but was strong in faith, giving glory to God; And being fully persuaded that, what he had promised, he was able also to perform."* (Romans 4:20-21) Unless otherwise, until there is **faith** in our heart, we cannot **"redeem our time."**

DECISION

A wise man once said that **decisions** are the **horses** we ride into **fame**—or into **shame**. In this life, we must make up our mind and on time, otherwise the devil will make up our time for us. *"Redeeming the time, because the days are evil."* (Ephesians 5:16)

If you do not make up your mind to work hard in life and succeed, you have planned to **fail in life**. *"And there were four leprous men at the entering in of the gate: and they said one to another, Why sit we here until we die? If we say, We will enter into the city, then the famine is in the city, and we shall die there: and if we sit still here, we die also. Now therefore come, and let us fall unto the host of the Syrians: if they save us alive, we shall live; and if they kill us, we shall but die."* (2 Kings 7:3-4)

Most of the things that happened in our lifetime are a function of decision. Decisions are the gateway into our freedom, liberty and a glorious future.

When you settle for less, you can only get what is entitled for the less privilege. (See Luke 16:21)

Despite all the riches of the father, the prodigal son took a drastic decision that reduced him to eat the pig's food, until he came to himself.
Luke 15:17

"In any moment of decision, the best thing you can do is the right thing. The worst thing you can do is nothing."
~Theodore Roosevelt

At every stage of our life, we constantly and continually make decisions that affect our future. If we are to "REDEEM OUR TIME," **we must make precise and accurate decisions about what we need to do going forward in life**.

PRAYER

But ye beloved, building up your selves on your most holy faith, praying in the Holy Ghost.
Jude 1:20

Prayer is a vital key to **redeem our time**, because prayer has no other alternative. **"A prayerless man is a useless man and a prayerless man is a hopeless man."** *"And he spake a parable unto them to this end, that men ought always to pray, and not to faint."* (Luke

18:1) The Bible says likewise, *"the Spirit also helpeth our infirmities; for we know not what we should pray for as we ought: but the Spirit itself maketh intercession for us with groaning which cannot be uttered."* (Romans 8:26) Most of the relief and confidence that will come into our life is by the assistance of the Holy Spirit in prayers. As believers, we are admonished that if we must **redeem our time**, we must be **prayerful in life**.

PRAYER POINT TO ACTIVATE THE PRESENCE OF THE HOLY SPIRIT

1) Holy Spirit, reveal yourself to me, in the name of Jesus.

2) Holy Spirit, crush every daily habit of sin, in the name of Jesus.

3) Holy Spirit, become my companion today, in the name of Jesus.

4) Holy Spirit, grant me access, in the name of Jesus.

5) Power of God, grant me the *grace* to live right for Jesus Christ.

6) Hand of God, deliver me from sin, in the name of Jesus.

7) Fire of God, burn every sinful thoughts from my mind, in the name of Jesus.

8) I proclaim authority over every prevailing sin in my life, in Jesus name.

9) I destroy every root of sin in my life, in Jesus name.

10) Sin shall not have dominion over my life, in the name of Jesus.

11) Lord God, emphasize genuine repentance over my Spirit man, in the name of Jesus

12) Holy Spirit, revive and rekindle your fire of revival inside of me, in the name of Jesus.

13) Power of God, hijack the controlling forces oppressing my life, in the name of Jesus.

14) Blood of Jesus, take over my life, in the name of Jesus.

15) O Lord, baptize me with the gift of the Holy Spirit.
16) Holy Spirit, breathe afresh upon my life, in the name of Jesus.

17) Holy Spirit, take possession of my will, in the name of Jesus.

18) Holy Spirit, make yourself real to me, in the name of Jesus.

19) Holy Spirit, fan your revival fire upon my life, in the name of Jesus.

CHAPTER 1
THE NUMBER OF YOUR DAYS

So teach us to number our days,
that we may apply our hearts unto wisdom
Psalms 90:12

Although our days are numbered, so many of us are living our lives as if there's an extra amount of time from God to be added unto our lives after we have wasted all our precious time here on earth. In our lifetime, every minute wasted will never be recovered. The Bible says in Ecclesiastes 3:1-2, *"To everything there is a season, and a time to every purpose under the heaven: A time to be born, and a time to die; a time to plant, and a time to pluck up that which is planted."*

I admonish you in the way of the Lord, *"in your lifetime, do not miss your time and your season,"* in Jesus name.

*To everything there is a season,
and a time to every purpose under the heaven:
A time to be born, and a time to die; a time to plant,
and a time to pluck up that which is planted;
A time to kill, and a time to heal; a time to break down,
and a time to build up; A time to weep, and a time to
laugh; a time to mourn, and a time to dance; A time to
cast away stones, and a time to gather stones together;
a time to embrace, and a time to refrain
from embracing;A time to get, and a time to lose;
a time to keep, and a time to cast away; A time to rend,
and a time to sew; a time to keep silence, and a time to
speak; A time to love, and a time to hate; a time of war,
and a time of peace. What profit hath he that worketh
in that wherein he laboureth.*
Ecclesiastes 3:1-9

What does it mean to "redeem the time?"

Acknowledge that you will never be here forever. With this in mind, we must transform and translate the way we reason, think and live. Ephesians 5:16 gives us a clear instruction and an absolute reason why we should **redeem** our time. *"Redeeming the time, because the days are evil."* The word "redeeming" in Greek means "to buy back, ransom or rescue from loss."

We must make efficient and effective use of every little bit of the time God gave us the privilege to enjoy. We can only redeem today and plan to redeem tomorrow, for our past is behind, our future is before us, our yesterday ended last night, and the best part of our life is yet to be lived. We are absolutely responsible for using what God has given to each of us—time—to prepare for our future.

WHY SHOULD WE REDEEM OUR TIME?

Because the days are evil.

Paul admonishes us to redeem the time because the days are evil. "Evil" in Greek means "hurtful, calamitous, diseased, derelict and vicious." We are living in the last days, in a terrific terrorist era, a time when building holy, righteous character is becoming increasingly difficult, if not impossible. Sin and the pleasure of immorality has overwhelmingly dominated the norm of the day. Redeem the time, because the days are evil. We live in an evil time. *"Sufficient unto the day is the evil thereof."* (Matthew 6:34)

FAILING TO NUMBER OUR DAYS

A lot of us, either by **neglect or ignorance**, live our life as if we will be here forever. Most of us **believers** do not meditate on the temporary state of human existence or that our days here are numbered. Human nature leads us to believe we will continue on, with unlimited physical days. This mindset permeates every new generation. *"So teach us to number our days, that we* *may apply our hearts unto wisdom."* (Psalms 90:12) As far as I know, we will all not be here forever. We must therefore take responsibility over our God-given time and make the most out of every minute, every hour, every day, every week, every month and every year.

The days of our years are threescore years and ten; and if by reason of strength they be fourscore years, yet is their strength labor and sorrow; for it is soon cut off, and we fly away.
Psalms 90:10

We all must spend our time wisely to maintain our physical existence and pursue our spiritual lives, for we will not be here forever. By this I mean we must work and make money to improve our lives. We must all become hard workers and not lazy people. *"For even when we were with you, this we commanded you, that if any would not work, neither should he eat."* (2 Theolossians 3:10)

PROCRASTINATION

A wise man once said that "procrastination is the mother of frustration." As long as we keep procrastinating, we will forever be in need and in want. *"I went by the field of the slothful, and by the vineyard of the man void of understanding; And, lo, it was all grown over with thorns, and nettles had covered the face thereof, and the stone wall thereof was broken down. Then I saw, and considered it well: I looked upon it, and received instruction. Yet a little sleep, a little slumber, a little folding of the hands to sleep: So shall thy poverty come as one that travelleth; and thy want as an armed man."* (Proverbs 24:30-34)

The only way to paralyze any great future is by putting it off! In my opinion, it is very unrealistic to procrastinate often. Procrastination is a sign of weakness and laziness. To some folks, it is natural to procrastinate—though not to me—to put off overcoming challenges, facing prevailing difficult decisions, changing poor study habits, praying for others, putting God's work first in life, etc. So many people delay life-changing decisions, settling for anxiety, unfulfilled goals, hopeless vision, frustrations and lack of accomplishment in life—all because of procrastination.

Procrastination causes us to inhibit creativity and postpone potential accomplishments that would lead to spiritual growth. We all face the pull of procrastination that hinders us of the time God has given us to overcome it. *"For he saith, I have heard thee in a time accepted, and in the day of salvation have I succoured thee: behold, now is the accepted time; behold, now is the day of salvation."* (2 Corinthians 6:2) There's never been a better time to confront our daily challenges than today. My mentor used to say, "What you failed to confront has power to conquer you."

WHAT IS SIN?

One man said S.I.N means Satan Identification Number. I do not disagree, but it is incomplete. In my own definition, sin is disobeying God's words and commandments. Every time you operate outside of the commandment of God, you are committing sin. *He that committeth sin is of the devil; for the devil sinneth from the beginning. For this purpose the son of God was manifested that he might destroy the works of the devil.* (1 John 3:8)

> *He that covereth his sins shall not prosper:*
> *but whoso confesseth and forsaketh them*
> *shall have mercy.*
> **Proverbs 28:13**

The pleasure and presence of sin in the life of the believer is a prevailing challenge for us all to keep up with our **salvation**.

> *Wherefore, my beloved, as ye have always obeyed, not*
> *as in my presence only, but now much more*
> *in my absence, work out your own salvation*
> *with fear and trembling.*
> **Philippians 2:12**

Whatever is not righteous before God and before man is sinful. Increasingly, the quest for sinful behavior is dominating and overwhelming us all in these evil times that we live in. The mind of humans has been greatly corrupted into evil and lustful behaviors. Most church folks can no longer differentiate between what is morally right or wrong and between what is ethically right or wrong. *"He that doeth righteousness is righteous, even as he is righteous."* (1 John 3:7)

David said it with clarity in Psalms 51:3: *"For I acknowledge my transgressions and my sin is ever before me."* We must not take the purpose of the life and death of Jesus in vain. Jesus Christ of Nazareth is a typical example for us all to follow his lifestyle. "Hereafter I will not talk much with you: for the prince of this world cometh, and hath nothing in me." (John 14:30)

WHO IS A SINNER?

*Behold I was shapen in iniquity;
and in sin did my mother conceive me*
Psalms 51:5

Although we were all born into sin, we have a choice to make in our lifetime. We can either decide to come out of sin—or die as sinners. *"I beseech you therefore, brethren, by the mercies of God, that ye present your bodies a living sacrifice, holy, acceptable unto God, which is your reasonable service. And be not conformed to this world: but be ye transformed by the renewing of your mind, that ye may prove what is that good, and acceptable, and perfect, will of God."* (Romans 12:1-2)

Besides knowing the commandment and understanding of the perfect will of God—and the demands for righteousness—the primary reason for the continuous preaching of the word of Gof is to constantly renew our mind from the attacks of the devil.

Examine yourselves, whether ye be in the faith;
prove your own selves. Know ye not your own selves,
how that Jesus Christ is in you, except ye be reprobates?
2 Corinthians 13:5

Although most faith people live in denial about the work of the flesh, from my own scriptural understanding, everyone operating within the scope of Galatians 5:20-21 is classified as a sinner.

Now the works of the flesh are manifest, which are these; Adultery, fornication, uncleanness, lasciviousness, idolatry, witchcraft, hatred, variance, emulations, wrath, strife, seditions, heresies, envyings, murders, drunkenness, revellings, and such like: of the which I tell you before, as I have also told you in time past, that they which do such things shall not inherit the kingdom of God.
Galatians 5:20-21

Further supporting scripture...

But the fearful, and unbelieving,
and the abominable, and murderers,
and whoremongers, and sorcerers, and idolaters,
and all liars, shall have their part in the lake
which burneth with fire and brimstone:
which is the second death.
Revelation 21:8

WHO, THEREFORE, IS A SINNER?

1) The Lazy Man: It is sinful for any able-bodied man or woman to fold their hands and make themselves beggars. The Bible says, *"the sluggard will not plow by reason of the cold; therefore shall he beg in harvest, and have nothing."* (Proverbs 20:4) In my own understanding, laziness is a sin. *For even when we were with you, this we commanded you, that if any would not work, neither should he eat.* (2 Thessalonians 3:10) \

Covenant mentality demands that we all understand that God has done His part over our lives. Jesus said I must work. It is dignified for every believer to earn money through the work of their hands—although most lazy people live in denial and tend to blame someone else. Nevertheless, Godliness demands that we take absolute responsibility for the outcome of our lives.

2) Unbelievers: In my view, all that have not acknowledged Jesus Christ as Lord and savior are sinners. The Bible says *God heareth not sinners*. Without contradiction, all unbelievers live in a sinful lifestyle. Unless God has mercy, most unbelievers will not make eternity in heaven.

3) Liars: All liars are sinners before the Almighty God. Lying is a very serious sin, simply because it leads to poverty and shame. Lying decays great destiny and erodes potential future. Someone who I know very well lies so much to themselves, they became a beggar by paralyzing their future and frustrating the will of God over their life.

HOW DO I COME OUT OF SIN?

*Know ye not, that to whom ye
yield yourselves servants to obey,
his servants ye are to whom ye obey;
whether of sin unto death,
or of obedience unto righteousness?*
Romans 6:16

In my opinion, it is hard for most people to come out of sin because of the excitement of the pleasure of sin. Take note! It is enjoying the pleasure of sin for a season that hinders even the very elect—those who have tasted the word of God.

*For it is impossible for those who were
once enlightened, and have tasted
of the heavenly gift, and were made partakers
of the Holy Ghost. And have tasted the good word of
God, and the powers of the world to come. If they shall
fall away, to renew them again unto repentance; seeing
they crucify to themselves the Son of God afresh, and
put him to an open shame*
Hebrews 6:4-6

We must be able to make a decision to come

out of sin. We must ***REPENT***, ***CONFESS*** and ***PROCLAIM*** the **LORD JESUS CHRIST.**

The word says as many as received him, to them gave He power to become the sons of God. Even to them that believe on his name.

To qualify for divine visitation, do the following (with sincerity):

1) ***Acknowledge*** that you are a sinner and that He died for you. (Romans 3:23)

2) ***Repent of your sins.*** (Acts 3:19, Luke 13:5, 2 Peter 3:9)

3) ***Believe in your heart*** that Jesus died for your sin. (Romans 10:10)

4) ***Confess Jesus as the Lord over your life.*** (Romans 10:10, Acts 2:21)

Now repeat this Prayer after me—

Say Lord Jesus, I accept you today, as my Lord and my savior, forgive me of my sins wash me with your blood. Right now, I believe, I am sanctified, I am save, I am free, I am free from the Power of sin to serve the Lord Jesus. Thank you Lord for saving me. Amen.

Congratulations.

YOU ARE NOW A BORN AGAIN CHRISTIAN!

STEPS TO OVERCOME THE LIFESTYLE OF SIN

FAITH

No one will overcome any sinful lifestyle without faith. Faith is the catalyst that will push you out of sin. Most prevailing controlling forces will not retreat unless the spirit of faith comes into play. Unless you develop faith, controlling forces have power to prevail. Therefore, develop faith that will crush all prevailing remote control forces. I see your faith bringing you deliverance over that prevailing lustful situation.

DECISIONS

Decisions are the wheels of destiny. Most of the things that happened in your lifetime are a function of decision. Decisions are the gateway into our freedom, liberty and a glorious future. When you settle for less, you can only get what is entitled for the less privilege. (See Luke 16:21). *"Despite all the riches of the father, the prodigal son took a drastic decision that reduced him to eat the pig's food, until he came to himself."* (Luke 15:17)

PRAYER

Prayer is a force of change that will overcome and dominate any obstacle harassing our destiny. The reason for all the calamities is because we are weak in

prayers. Prayer is a pillar of destiny. As far as I know, nothing changes within you until you **pray** about it. Every time we pray, we must depend upon the HOLY SPIRIT. We must therefore activate the person and presence of the Holy Spirit in our lives.

HOW TO ACTIVATE THE HOLY SPIRIT IN YOUR LIFE

First of all, you must believe that there is a Holy Spirit.

1) *Acknowledge* the person of the Holy Spirt.

2) *Believe* in the ministration of the Holy Spirit.

3) *Submit & obey* the person of the Holy Spirit.

4) *Welcome* the sweet presence of the Holy Spirit.

Begin a relationship with the Holy Spirit today and make Him your best friend. Never start your day without inviting the person of the Holy Spirit to come into your life.

SUMMARY OF CHAPTER ONE

THE NUMBER OF YOUR DAYS

For all our days are passed away in thy wrath:
we spend our years as a tale that is told.
The days of our years are threescore years and ten;
and if by reason of strength they be fourscore years,
yet is their strength labour and sorrow;
for it is soon cut off, and we fly away.
James 5:13-16

We must understand that we won't be here forever. Thus, we must take advantage of our God-given time. Ben Franklin once said, "Dost thou love life? Then do not squander time, for that's the stuff life is made of." Our greatest access is our time. We must maximize the use of it to our profiting. Everyone has 24 hours in one day. A lot of us work and desire to do more "over time." It is not overtime that will make you rich, but **the blessing of the Lord**. We must therefore desire to follow our **God's calling** in our life.

We must be disciplined in life and we must understand that there is a time for everything in life. *"To everything there is a season, and a time to every purpose under the heaven: A time to be born, and a time to die; a time to plant, and a time to pluck up that which is planted; A time to kill, and a time to heal; a time to break down, and a time to build up; A time to weep, and a time to laugh; a time to mourn, and a time to dance."* (Ecclesiastes 3:1-4)

Finally we must take advantage of our time for **time is money**. *"Whatsoever thy hand findeth to do, do it with thy might; for there is no work, nor device, nor knowledge, nor wisdom, in the grave, whither thou goest."*

(Ecclesiastes 9:10)

CHAPTER 2
INVESTING YOUR TIME

Whatsoever thy hand findeth to do, do it with thy might; for there is no work, nor device, nor knowledge, nor wisdom, in the grave, whither thou goest
Ecclesiastes 9:10

Most successful men and women I have known here in the United States of America started pursuing their vision when they were very young in life. We must all become conscious of our God-given time. A great man once said "TIME IS MONEY."

"We must use time creatively, and forever realize that the time is always ripe to do right."
~Nelson Mandela

Everyone must start pursing their God-given "VISON" early in life. If we are to become successful in our lifetime, we must work hard towards becoming successful in life. Success, therefore, is not by luck or by wishing.

Collin Powell said, "There are no secrets to success: don't waste time looking for them. Success is the result of perfection, hard work, learning from failure, loyalty to those for whom you work and persistence."

Jesus Christ made a profound statement about productive work when he said, *"I must work the works of him that sent me, while it is day: the night cometh, when no man can work."* (John 9:4)

Hezekiah lamented in Isaiah 38:10-13, *"I said in the cutting off of my days, I shall go to the gates of the grave: I am deprived of the residue of my years. I said, I shall not see the Lord, even the Lord, in the land of the living: I shall behold man no more with the inhabitants of the world. Mine age is departed, and is removed from me as a shepherd's tent: I have cut off like a weaver my life: he will cut me off with pining sickness: from day even to night wilt thou make an end of me. I reckoned till morning, that, as a lion, so will he break all my bones: from day even to night wilt thou make an end of me."* (Romans 8:26)

We must identify the area of our calling and pursue it. We must not allow friends and environmental challenges to adversely influence our lives.

For there is no difference between the Jew and the Greek: for the same Lord over all is rich unto all that call upon him.
Romans 10:12

GOD is for all, both the rich and the poor. *"The rich and poor meet together: the Lord is the maker of them all."* (Proverbs 22:2) As long as we do the will of God, God will bless and multiply us abundantly. *"Then Peter opened his mouth, and said, Of a truth I perceive that God is no respecter of persons: But in every nation he that feareth him, and worketh righteousness, is accepted with him."* (Acts 10:34-35)

We must therefore invest our time wisely. We must take advantage of every little opportunity that comes our way in life. *"Submit yourselves therefore to God. Resist the devil, and he will flee from you."* (James 4:7)

Lets's briefly examine the HOLY GHOST:

CONCLUSION OF CHAPTER 2

ISufficient unto the day is the evil thereof.
Matthew 6:34

We must invest our time wisely. Acknowledge with me that you do not have a spare life. I encourage you to never settle for less in your lifetime. *"But the path of the just is as the shining light, that shineth more and more unto the perfect day."* (Proverbs 4:18)

If you are employed, do not quit your job—but keep looking for something better than your current job position. Always have a big plan for your life.

1) Never allow circumstances to manipulate your life.

2) Always believe you can do better.

3) Appreciate life and spend time with your loved ones.

4) Never give up in life. Enjoy every single moment.

5) Winner do not quit.

6) Believers do not quit.

7) Never be afraid for any reason in life.

8) Always be conscious of the hand of God in your life.

9) Always take advantage of your time.

CHAPTER 3
MAXIMIZING OUR POTENTIAL

For I would that all men were even as I myself. But every man hath his proper gift of God, one after this manner, and another after that.
1 Corinthians 7:7

In these end times, everybody wants to be heard, noticed and appreciated. Almost all of us are eager and anxious for fame and celebrity status. As a result of hasty decisions, we end up in the wrong business or career. *"He that believeth shall not make haste."* (Isaiah 28:16)

As long as we can acknowledge that we will not live forever, we must take advantage of every moment of our life. We must maximize our God-given time. We must invest our time in meaningful and impactful work. I have seen great men—talented, too—who could have become journalists, editors, even writers, waste their lives as security guards. Prevailing circumstances around you may narrow your life into a security office job—but that does not mean you must settle in that job forever. *"Wherefore he saith, Awake thou that sleepest, and arise from the dead, and Christ shall give thee light."* (Ephesians 5:14)

WE MUST APPRECIATE THAT WE ARE ALL CALLED BY GOD

My Bible tells me that your **gift** will make room for you and your **gift** will bring you before men. *"A man's gift maketh room for him, and bringeth him before great men."* (Proverbs 18:16)

*But as God hath distributed to every man,
as the Lord hath called every one, so let him walk.
And so ordain I in all churches.*
1 Corinthians 7:17

WE MUST DISCOVER OUR AREA OF CALLING BY GOD

*Let every man abide in the same calling
wherein he was called*
1 Corinthians 7:20

WE MUST STAY IN OUR OWN AREA OF CALLING BY GOD

*Brethren, let every man, wherein he is called,
therein abide with God.*
1 Corinthians 7:24

Although so many of us live in denial, the **Holy Bible** supports my argument that we are all called by God. The Bible says, *"For many are called, but few are chosen."* (Matthew 22:14) We must all awake and understand our uniqueness and calling in Christ Jesus. As long as we recognize our calling in Christ Jesus, we will be successful in life.

A man's gift maketh room for him,
and bringeth him before great men.
Proverbs 18:16

MAXIMIZING YOUR POTENTIAL

It is not hard work that makes a man—but **meaningful** work. We must all look for what we love to do and embrace it as our calling in life. *"Labour not to be rich: cease from thine own wisdom Jesus said. I must work the works of him that sent me, while it is day: the night cometh, when no man can work. Whatsoever thy hand findeth to do, do it with thy might; for there is no work, nor device, nor knowledge, nor wisdom, in the grave, whither thou goest."* (Ecclesiastes 9:10)

But ye are a chosen generation, a royal priesthood,
an holy nation, a peculiar people; that ye should shew
forth the praises of him who hath called you
out of darkness into his marvellous light.
1 Peter 2:9

We must not frustrate the grace of God upon our lives. We are absolutely responsible for the outcome of our lives. I admonish you to stop the blame game and take responsibility for the outcome of your life.

DISCOVER THE CALL OF GOD OVER YOUR LIFE AND PURSUE IT WITHOUT WASTING TIME

We must therefore engage our heart and our hand in meaningful, but impactful, work. Living without working is dying without knowing. Do not trouble you heart by what you lost in the past.

Apostle Paul said, *"Brethren, I count not myself to have apprehended: but this one thing I do, forgetting those things which are behind, and reaching forth unto those things which are before, I press toward the mark for the prize of the high calling of God in Christ Jesus. Let us therefore, as many as be perfect, be thus minded: and if in anything ye be otherwise minded, God shall reveal even this unto you."* (Philippians 3:13)

- —If you are DEPRESSED, you are living in the PAST.

- —If you are ANXIOUS, you are living in the FUTURE.

—But if you are AT PEACE, you are living in the PRESENT.

HEALING KEYS

1) Always carry a positive mindset, regardless of the prevailing circumstances.

2) Always tell yourself the truth before you lie about it.

3) If the truth be told, you are a branch of His blessings, the planting of the Lord.

4) Never confess that you are sick to the hearing of the member of your body.

5) Positive confession with faith yields positive results.

6) Every cures of man have no power to prevail over your life.

7) A merry heart is medicinal and health to your body.

8) Spiritual and emotional well-being is vital to happiness in life.

9) To avoid depression, never have regrets.

10) Never be anxious in life to avoid anxiety.

11) Always live today for today to be at peace with your spirit and with God.

11) You're unique because your challenges are tailored to you only.

12) The blessing always dominates the curses any day.

13) Decisions are the wheels of life.

14) We either ride into fame or into shame.

15) Daily exercise and some reading of the Bible gurantees good health.

16) Every day is God's day. No day created by God is a disapointment.

17) Stay away from sweet stuff—they are temporary.

18) Sugar is sweet to your taste, beware! It also contributes to diabetes.

19) A good prayer life gurantees longivity.

20) People that pray in tongues do not develop mental disease.

21) Always be positive in everything.

22) Always have a mentor in life that will oppose and fight the tormentor.

23) Always have someone in life to learn from.

24) Tell everybody what you plan to do and someone will help you do it.

25) Winners fight to the last.

26) Quitters never win in life.

27) Soul winners are heirs to the kingdom of god.

28) Soul winners never lack help.

29) Soul winners are cerified with divine help.

30) God is always looking for soul winners to bless.

31) Life is a warfare and not a funfare.

32) In life you fight for all you possess.

33) No man or woman was born rich.

34) In your lifetime do something positive to impact your world.

35) Take care of your life today—you don't have one

to spare.

36) Take your life serious before the devil take you down.

37) Always be cheerful at all times.

38) Regardless of the prevailing circumstances around you, your life is in the hand of God.

39) God is the super surgeon that will spiritually-surgically heal you.

40) Always expect help from above and not from abroad.

41) Man will disappoint you, but god will appoint you.

42) The joy of the lord is always our strength.

43) Spiritual height is not measured in length or breath.

44) If you go deeper with God, you will see deeper.

45) Your next level in life is full of recognition.

46) Go to where you are celebrated and not where you are tolerated.

47) Develop yourself in the area of your calling in life.

48) A lifestyle of thanks given keeps God 24/7 on duty on our behalf.

49) Develop a lifestyle of thanksgiving.

50) Thanksgiving gurantees our access to obtain the promises.

DECISION KEYS

1) Nothing changes until you make up your mind.

2) Decision is the gateway to deliverance.

3) Until you decide, no one will decide for you.

4) Your prosperity is proportional to your decisions.

5) The decision you make will determine the future you will create

6) Decision creates future and fulfills destinies.

7) Decision beautifies our future.

8) Decision keeps you out of trouble.

9) Decision exempts you from evil.

10) Decision gurantees eternity.

11) You can only go far in life by your faith decisions.

12) You are poor because you made such decisions

13) Make a decision and change your life.

14) Life changing decisions are a function of quality information.

15) Success in life is a function of decision.

16) Life experiences are full of decisions.

17) Decisions change destinies.

18) Never settle for information—always look for revelation.

19) You are where you are today based on your last decision.

20) Information is crucial in decision making.

21) Decision makers rule the world.

22) You can rule your world with quality decisions.

23) As long as you decide rightly, Satan cannot harrass

you.

PRAYER POINTS TO OVERCOME TRIALS BY THE HELP OF THE HOLY SPIRIT

1) Father Lord, deliver me from this present trial, in the name of Jesus.

2) Almighty Father, break me out of this present obscurity, in the name of Jesus.

3) Holy Spirit, help me to overcome this trial, in Jesus name.

4) Holy Spirit, speak to me, in the name of Jesus.

5) Holy Spirit, minister to my subconscious spirit, in the name of Jesus.

6) Fire of God, burn down every mountain of difficulty, in the name of Jesus.

7) Holy Ghost, baptize me with your fire, in the name of Jesus.

8) Holy Spirit, go before me and favor me in this present challenge, in the name of Jesus.

9) Spirit of God, grant me liberty and freedom by the

fire of the Holy Spirit, in the name of Jesus.

10) Father Lord, intervene on my behalf, in the name of Jesus.

11) Ancient of day, liberate me this season, in the name of Jesus.

12) Immortal redeemer, bring me higher above these prevailing changes.

13) Lord God, turn this present obstacale into my miracle, in the name of Jesus.

14) Fire of God, break down these obstacles for me, in the name of Jesus.

15) Holy Spirit, favor me in, Jesus name.

16) Holy Spirit. release me from this challenge, in the name of Jesus.

17) Holy Spirit, become my compionion, in Jesus name.

18) Holy Spirit, represent me in this matter.

19) Holy Spirit, elevant me beyond my own immagination, in the name of Jesus.

20) Holy Spirit, do not allow my enemies to truimph over my life, in the name of Jesus.

21) Fire of God, protect me, in the name of Jesus.

22) Fire of God, destroy my enemies, in the name of Jesus.

23) Fire of God, build a wall around me, in the name of Jesus.

24) Fire of God, expose my enemies, in the name of Jesus.

25) Fire of God, prove yourself, in the name of Jesus.

26) Holy Spirit, represent me in jesus name.

27) Holy Spirit, release your boldnes into my life.

28) Holy Spirit, grant me signs and wonders.

29) Holy Spirit, make me a living wonder in my lifetime.

30) Holy Spirit, turn my life around, in the name of Jesus.

31) Holy Spirit, I will not remain at this level, in the name of Jesus.

32) Spirit of God, lift me higher, in the mighty name of Jesus.

33) Angels of God, minister unto me, in the name of

Jesus.

34) Hand of God, separate me this season, in the name of Jesus.

CONCLUSION

Redeeming the time, because the days are evil. Wherefore be ye not unwise, but understanding what the will of the Lord is.
Ephesians 5:16-17

What are we saying in a book like this?

You *must* take advantage of your God-given time. Remember Benjamin Franklin once said, "*time is money*." Always strive to make the best out of every day, every week, every month and every year. The Bible says, *"Whatsoever thy hand findeth to do, do it with thy might; for there is no work, nor device, nor knowledge, nor wisdom, in the grave, whither thou goest."* (Ecclesiastes 9:10) A lot of us Christians complain and blame others for being responsible for their failures. In my opinion, you are absolutely and completely esponsible for the outcome of your life.

Sufficient unto the day is the evil thereof.
Matthew 6:34

There are no evil forces holding us hostage. Most of us are mental prisoners. We imprisoned our life by frustrating the **will of God** for our lives. I admonish you in the **name of the Lord**, do not subject yourself to the will of the devil. The devil has **no power over your life.** *"Shake thyself from the dust; arise, and sit down, O Jerusalem: loose thyself from the bands of thy neck, O captive daughter of Zion. For thus saith the Lord, Ye have sold yourselves for nought; and ye shall be redeemed without money."* (Isaiah 52:2-3)

As long as you have made up your mind to do something positive with your time, with faith in your heart, God is obligated to honor you. *"Let thy work appear unto thy servants, and thy glory unto their children. And let the beauty of the Lord our God be upon us: and establish thou the work of our hands upon us; yea, the work of our hands establish thou it."* (Psalms 90:16-17)

Wherefore he saith, Awake thou that sleepest, and arise from the dead, and Christ shall give thee light.
Ephesians 5:14

BIBLICAL PERSONALITIIES TO INSPIRE YOU

JOSEPH

Joseph, the son of Jacob—who was despised by his brothers in his father's home—was later thrown into a pit. In his teenage days he became a slave at Potiphar's house and ended up in prison. (See Genesis 37:20, Genesis 39:2, Genesis 39:21, Genesis 41:39-14) At the age of 30 he appeared before the king and was greatly honored.

MOSES

How about the life of Moses? *"By faith Moses, when he was come to years, refused to be called the son of Pharaoh's daughter; Choosing rather to suffer affliction with the people of God, than to enjoy the pleasures of sin for a season."* (Hebrew 11:24-25) The life story of a man like Moses should inspire us all. He was a murderer who ran away for a period of 40 years. Moses became a celebrity in the land of Egypt and was very famous in the nation of Israel, all because he was faithful to the calling of GOD upon his life.

DANIEL

How about the life of the man named Daniel? *"This Daniel was preferred above the presidents and princes, because an excellent spirit was in him; and the king thought to set him over the whole realm."* (Daniel 6:3) This man Daniel survived inside of the lion's den. Daniel, a man of decision, a man who made up his mind concerning God. *"But Daniel purposed in his heart that he would not defile himself with the portion of the king's meat, nor with the wine which he drank: therefore he requested of the prince of the eunuchs that he might not defile himself."* (Daniel 1:8)

PAUL

How about the life of Paul? A trained lawyer who turned around his time to do the **will of God.** A man who was beaten and thrown into prison. (See Acts 16:19-25.) This is what Paul himself had to say: *"Of the Jews five times received I forty stripes save one. Thrice was I beaten with rods, once was I stoned, thrice I suffered shipwreck, a night and a day I have been in the deep; In journeyings often, in perils of waters, in perils of robbers, in perils by mine own countrymen, in perils by the heathen, in perils in the city, in perils in the wilderness, in perils in the sea, in perils among false brethren; In weariness and painfulness, in watchings often, in hunger and thirst, in fastings often, in cold and nakedness."* (2 Corinthians 11:24-27)

There is a great future for you—if only you will make up your mind to do the **will of God.** You must there discover your talent and pursue the **will of God** concerning your life. **Redeem your time while you are still alive**!

> *Let us hear the conclusion of the whole matter:*
> *Fear God, and keep his commandments:*
> *for this is the whole duty of man.*
> *For God shall bring every work into judgment,*
> *with every secret thing, whether it be good,*
> *or whether it be evil*
> **Ecclesiastes 12:13-14**

It takes a change of heart to have a change of life. Nothing changes around or within you until you change your heart. The Bible says in Ecclesiastes

12:14, *"For God shall bring every work into judgment, with every secret thing, whether it be good, or whether it be evil."* If you are a born again Christian, we'd like to encourage you in your Christian life. If you are not a born again Christian, we can help you receive genuine salvation right here. *"Therefore if any man be in Christ, he is a new creature: old things are passed away; behold, all things are become new."* (2 Corinthians 5:17)

Now repeat this prayer after me:

Say Lord Jesus, I accept you today, as my Lord and my savior. Forgive me of my sins, wash me with your blood. Right now, I believe I am sanctified, I am saved, I am free. I am free from the power of sin, to serve the Lord Jesus. Thank you Lord for saving me. Amen.

Congratulations. You are now...

A BORN AGAIN CHRISTIAN.

Again I say to you—CONGRATULATIONS!

What must I do to determine my divine visitation?

To determine divine visitation you must be born again! The word says as many as received him, to them gave He power to become the sons of God. Even to them that believe on his name.

To qualify for divine visitation,

do the following sincerely:

1) Acknowledge that you are a sinner and that He died for you. (Romans 3:23)
2) Repent of your sins. (Acts 3:19, Luke 13:5, 2 Peter 3:9)

3) Believe in your heart that Jesus died for your sin. (Romans 10:10)

4) Confess Jesus as the Lord over your life. (Romans 10:10, Acts 2:21)

NOW REPEAT THIS PRAYER AFTER ME:
Say Lord Jesus, I accept you today, as my Lord and my savior, forgive me of my sins wash me with your blood. Right now, I believe, I am sanctified, I am save, I am free, I am free from the Power of sin to serve the Lord Jesus. Thank you Lord for saving me. Amen.

Congratulations.

YOU ARE NOW A BORN AGAIN CHRISTAIN!

Again, I say to you—congratulations!

I adjure you to watch the Spirit of God bear witness with your Spirit confirming His word with signs following. The word says the Spirit itself beareth witness with our spirit, that we are the children of God.

Join a bible believing church or join us on our weekly and Sunday worship services at 343 Sanford Avenue Newark New Jersey 07106.

WISDOM KEYS

— Every productive society is a society heading to the top.

—Millions of Nigerians run away from Nigeria. Very few Nigerians stay in Nigeria.

—My decision to return Nigeria is the will of God for my life.

—My shortcoming in America after 18 years is the fact that I've trained me to be wise, to think, reflect and reason appropriately.

—If you train your mind to reason, it will train your hands to earn money.

—It is absurd to use the money of the heathen to build the kingdom of the living God.

—Every ministry reveals its agenda and VISION either at the beginning or at the end.

—Be careful of your life. It is your first ministry.

—The average American mind is conditioned for a continual quest to get new things and discard the old.

—When I considered well, my BMW jeep became my initial deposit for the work of the ministry in Nigeria.

—Money will never fall from any tree or person. Make up your mind to be independent today.

—Everyone is waiting for you to change your mind. Until you change your thinking, nothing changes around you.

—Multiple academic degrees in other disciplines gave me the chance to think and reason.

—Whatever anyone is thinking at any time reveals what is inside of their heart.

—All planned events are the product of meditation.

—Every event is designed for a designated timeline.

—Wisdom is your ability to think, to create and invent.

— If you can think wisely enough, you will come out of debt.

—The distance between you and your success is your innovative and creative ability to think well.

—Success is the result of hard work, commitment, resolve and determined learning from past mistakes and failings.

—If you organize your mind, you have organized your life and destiny.

—There is a thin line between success and failure.

—Wealth is your ability to think, power is your ability to reason and success is your ability to be informed.

—If you can make use of your mind by thinking and reasoning, God will make use of your life and destiny.

—Reflect, reason, think and be Great.

—Famous people are born of woman.

—That you will make it is your intention, that you will survive is your resolve, that you will succeed with changes is your determination, personal efforts and hard work.

—No man was born a failure.

—Lack of vision is the result of failure.

—Working with mental patients encourages and aspire me to be a productive observant and dedicated to my assignment.

—Successful people are not magicians. It is the willpower, combined with hard work and determination and a resolve to succeed, that make them succeed.

—In the unequivocal state of the mind, intention is not a location or a position. It is the state of the mind.

—So many people think that they think.

—The mind is used to think, to reflect and to reason.

—You will remain blind with your eyes open until you can see with your mind by thinking.

—There is no favoritism in accurate and precise calculation.

—Although knowledge is power, information is the key and gateway to a great future.

—It will take the hand of God to move the hand of man.

—With the backing of the great wise God, nothing will disconnect you from your inheritance.

—As long as you have wisdom and understanding of God, Satan and evil cannot manipulate your life and destiny.

—You have come this far in life by your own judgment and the decisions you made in the past. Now lean in and listen to God for another dimension of greatness.

—Great people are ordinary people. It is extra ordinary efforts and the price of sacrifice that produces greatness in them.

—As a mental direct care worker, I saw a great pastor and a motivational speaker within myself.

—A menial job does not reduce your self-worth. Until you resolve to achieve greatness and see greatness in all you do, you will never count in your community.

—The principle of Jesus will solve your gambling and addiction problems.

—The man of Jesus will lead you into heaven.

—Everyone has their self-appraisal and what they think about you. Until you discover yourself, other opinions about you will alter the real you.

—Supervisors and directors are just a position in the chain of command in a workplace. Never allow your supervisor hierarchy to alter your opinion of yourself.

—Everyone can come out of debt if they make up their mind.
—The fact that I am not a decision-maker at work does not diminish my contribution to my world.

—Although it appears like it was a poor decision to accept a direct care employment at a psychiatric hospital, as I reflect on my nine years of that experience, it became apparent that I have learned and experienced enough for my next assignment.

—Self-encouragement and determination is a resolve of the heart.

—If you are determined to make a difference and do the things that make a difference, you will eventually make a difference.

—Good things do not come easy.

—Short cuts will cut your life short.

—Those who look ahead move ahead.

—Life is all about making an impact. In your lifetime strive to make an impact in your community.

—Make friends and connect with people who are moving ahead of you in life.

—If you can look around well, you have come a long way in your life, made a lot of difference and realized a lot of success in life.

—If you are my old friend, hurry up to reach out to me before I become a stranger to you.

—I am blessed with inspirations from God that changed my interpretation of the world around me.

—I thought I was stagnant and lonely until I looked around and noticed my children running around and my wife cooking.

— At 40, I resigned my job to seek the Lord forever.

—My ministry took a drastic rise to the top when the wisdom of God visited me with knowledge and understanding.

—You will be a better person if you understand the characteristics of your personality like your mood swings, attitudes and habits.

—It is the seed of love you sow into the heart of a child and a woman that you reap in due time.

—Love is not selfish. Love shares everything, including the concealed secrets of the mind.

—As long as you have a prayer life and a Bible, you will never feel lonely in the race of life.
—When good friends disconnect from you, let them go. They might have seen something new in a different direction.

—Confidence in yourself and in God is the only way to bring you out of captivity

—Never train a child to waste his or her time.

—The mind is the greatest asset of a great future.

—You walk by common sense, run by principles and fly by instruction.

—Those who become successful in life did it by self-determination, hard work and learning from past failures.

—Most successful people are lonely people. No one renders help to them, believing they are already successful. Except when they seek for more knowledge and information, they are all alone.

— I have seen a towing truck vehicle. I have also seen a towing ship in the water. But I have never seen a towing airplane in the air.

—I exercise my judgment and make a decision every minute of the day. Decisions are crucial, critical and vital with reference to your future.

—So many people wish for a great future. You can only work towards a great future.

—Your celebrity status began when you discovered your talent. What are you good at? Work at it with all your commitment.

—Prayers will sustain you, but the wisdom of God will prosper you.

—When I met Oyedepo, his teachings changed my perspective. But when I met Ibiyeomie, his teachings changed my perception.

— I will be successful in ministry if only I concentrate and focus my energy in the work of the ministry.

— It took the late Dr. Norman Vincent Peale's book to open my mind towards the kingdom of success.

CHAPTER 4
PRAYER OF SALVATION

"SALVATION" simply implies **deliverance** and **rescue** of our soul, **body** and **spirit** from **sin** and **sickness** and **diseases**. There is only one way and in one name through which we can experience genuine salvation. Salvation is only possible in the name of **Jesus Christ**. *"Neither is there salvation in any other: for there is none other name under heaven given among men, whereby we must be saved."* (Acts 4:12)

I want you, if you have not given your life to Jesus already, to do so now. Give your life to Christ. I want you to know the truth! The truth is that Jesus died for your sins. And because He died, you must be **saved, alive and free!**

What must I do to truly experiene genuine **SALVATION**?

To experience **salvation** we must **believe on his name** and we must be born again! The word says, *"as many as received Him, to them gave He power to become the sons of God. Even to them that believe on his name."* (John 1:12)

To qualify for **salvation**, do the following with sincerity—

> 1) Acknowledge that you are a sinner and that He died for you. (Romans 3:23)
> 2) Repent of your sins. (Acts 3:19, Luke 13:5, 2 Peter 3:9)
> 3) Believe in your heart that Jesus died for your sins. (Romans 10:10)
> 4) Confess Jesus as the Lord over your life. (Romans 10:10, Acts 2:21)

Now repeat this prayer after me:

Say Lord Jesus, I accept you today, as my Lord and my savior. Forgive me of my sins, wash me with your blood. Right now, I believe I am sanctified, I am saved, I am free. I am free from the power of sin, to serve the Lord Jesus. Thank you Lord for saving me. Amen.

Congratulations. You are now...

A BORN AGAIN CHRISTIAN.

Again I say to you—CONGRATULATIONS!

I adjure you to watch the Spirit of God bear witness with your Spirit, confirming His word with signs following. The word says The Spirit itself beareth witness with our spirit, that we are the children of God.

MIRACLE CARE OUTREACH

"...But that the members should have the same care one for another"
1 Corinthians 12:25

We are all members of the body of Christ. Jesus commanded us to love our neighbor as ourselves. This includes caring for one another as a member of one body. True love is expressed in caring and giving. The word says, for God so Love He gave....

Reach out to someone in need of Jesus. Help someone in crisis find Christ. Look out and prove your love to Jesus by caring and inviting your friends and associates to find Jesus the Healer.

Invite your friends to our Home Care Cell Fellowship (Miracle Chapel Intl. Satellite Fellowship). We're in the U.S. at 33 Schley Street, Newark, New Jersey 07112. Home Care Cell Fellowship Group meets every Tuesday at 6:00pm-7:00pm.

If you are in Nigeria—MIRACLE OF GOD MINISTRIES, aka "MIRACLE CHAPEL INTL." Mpama–Egbu-Owerri Imo state Nigeria.

LIFE IS NOT ALL ABOUT DURATION,

BUT IT'S ALL ABOUT DONATION

What does this statement mean?

Life consists not in accumulation of material wealth. (Luke 12:15) But it's all about liberality…i.e., what you can give and share with others. (Proverbs 11:25) When you live for others, you live forever—because you outlive your generation by the legacy you leave behind after you depart into glory to be with the Lord. But when you live for yourself, when you are reduced to SELF—you are easily forgotten when you die and depart in glory.

Permit me to admonish you today to live your life to be a blessing to a soul connected to you today. I want you to know that so many souls are connected and looking up to you, and through you so many souls will be saved and rescued from destruction. Will you disciple someone today to find Jesus Christ?

As a genuine Christian, it is your duty to evangelize Jesus Christ to all you meet on your way. Jesus is still in the healing business—Jesus is still doing miracles, from time of old to now. Therefore, tell someone about Jesus Christ today, disciple and bring them to Church. *Philip findeth Nathanael...* (John 1:45)

Please prove the sincerity of your love for God today, please become a soul winner. The dignity of your Christianity is hidden in your boldness to proclaim and evangelize Jesus Christ to all you meet on your way. There is a question mark on the integrity of your Christianity until you become a life soul winner. Invite someone to join us worship the Lord Jesus this coming Sunday. Amen.

MIRACLE OF GOD MINISTRIES
PILLARS OF THE COMMISSION

We Believe, Preach and Practice the following:

1) We believe and preach Salvation to every living human being.

2) We believe and preach Repentance and Forgiveness of sins.

3) We believe and preach the baptism of the Holy Spirit and Spiritual gifts.

4) We believe and teach Prosperity.

5) We believe and preach Divine Healing and Miracles—Signs and Wonder.

6) We believe and preach Faith.

7) We believe and proclaim the Power of God (Supernatural).

8) We believe and proclaim Praise and Worship to God.

9) We believe and preach Wisdom.
10) We believe and preach Holiness (Consecration).

11) We believe and preach Vision.

12) We believe and teach the Word of God.

13) We believe and teach Success.

14) We believe and practice Prayer.

15) We believe and teach Deliverance.

These 15 stones form the Pillars of Our Commission. Become part of this church family and follow this great move of God.

MY HEARTFELT PRAYER FOR YOU

It is my burning desire for God to touch you through one of our teaching books or CDs. It also my personal desire for you encounter God for yourself.

Now let me Pray for you:

O Lord God! I beseech thee, and through personal prayer intercession today that the Holy Spirit will touch the precious soul reading this book and turn their life around. Spirit of God, possess this loved one. Lord, overcome all dominating, controlling forces that have prevailed over their lives. I come against all oppressive thought, in Jesus name. Henceforth, I pronounce you free from manipulation, intimidation and domination of the wicked enemy called the devil. You are free from all satanic harassment and assaults. Amen.

TIME TO TURN TO GOD

Have you ever ask why are you here? God planted you here to bring to pass his plan over your life

The best of your physical strength and efforts is the beginning of God's grace.

Eternity is real, heaven is sure. Become interested in the heavenly race and book your name in the lamb book of life.

"Everything great comes by his grace upon your life. Therefore turn unto God in suplication, in thanksgiving and in prayer, and god will turn in your favor." (Philippians 4:6)

ABOUT THE AUTHOR

Rev. Franklin N. Abazie is the founding and Presiding Pastor of Miracle of God Ministries, with headquarters in Newark, New Jersey USA and a branch church in Owerri-Imo State Nigeria. He is following the footsteps of one of his mentors, the healing evangelist Oral Roberts of the blessed memory. The Lord passed Oral Roberts' healing mantle two days before he went to be with the Lord at age 91 into the hands of healing evangelist Rev. Franklin N. Abazie in a vision.

In all his services, the Power and Presence of God is present to heal all in his audience. Rev. Abazie is an ordained man of God, with a Healing Ministry reviving the healing and miracle ministry of Jesus Christ of Nazareth.

Pastor Franklin N. Abazie, has been called by God with a unique mandate: **"THE MOMENT IS DUE TO IMPACT YOUR WORLD THROUGH THE REVIVAL OF THE HEALING AND MIRACLE MINISTRY OF JESUS CHRIST OF NAZA-**

RETH.

"I AM SENDING YOU TO RESTORE HEALTH UNTO THEE AND I WILL HEAL THEE OF THY WOUNDS, SAID THE LORD OF HOST"

Rev. Abazie is a gifted, ardent teacher of the word of God, who operates also in the office of a Prophet, generating and attracting undeniable signs and wonders, special miracles and healings, with apostolic fireworks of the Holy Ghost. He is the founding and presiding senior Pastor of this fast growing Healing Ministry. He has written over 86 inspirational, healing and transforming books covering almost all aspects of divine healing and life. He is happily married and blessed with children.

BOOKS BY REV. FRANKLIN N. ABAZIE:

1) The Outcome of Faith
2) Understanding the Secret of Prevailing Prayers
3) Commanding Abundance
4) Understanding the Secret of the Man God Uses
5) Activating My Due Season
6) Overcoming Divine Verdicts
7) The Outcome of Divine Wisdom
8) Understanding God's Restoration Mandate
9) Walking In the Victory and Authority of the Truth
10) God's Covenant Exemption
11) Destiny Restoration Pillars
12) Provoking Acceptable Praise
13) Understanding Divine Judgment
14) Activating Angelic Re-enforcement
15) Provoking Un-Merited Favo
16) The Benefits of the Speaking Faith
17) Understanding Divine Arrangement
18) How to Keep Your Healing
19) Understanding the Mysteries of the Speaking Faith
20) Understanding the Mysteries of Prophetic Healing
21) Operating Under the Rules of Creative Healing
22) Understanding the Joy of Breakthrough
23) Understanding the Mystery of Breakthrough
24) Understanding Divine Prosperity
25) Understanding Divine Healing

26) Retaining Your Inheritance
27) Overcoming Confusing Spirit
28) Commanding Angelic Escorts
29) Enforcing Your Inheritance In Christ Jesus
30) Understanding Your Guardian Angels
31) Overcoming the Dominion of Sin
32) Understanding the Voice of God
33) The Outstanding Benefits of the Anointing
34) The Audacity of the Blood of Jesus
35) Walking in the Reality of the Anointing
36) Escaping the Nightmare of Poverty
37) Understanding Your Harvest Season
38) Activating Your Success Buttons
39) Overcoming the Forces of Darkness
40) Overcoming the Devices of the Devil
41) Overcoming Demonic Agents
42) Overcoming the Sorrows of Failure
43) Rejecting the Sorrows of Failure
44) Resisting the Sorrows of Poverty
45) Restoring Broken Marriages
46) Redeeming Your Days
47) The Force of Vision
48) Overcoming the Forces of Ignorance
49) Understanding the Sacrifice of Small Beginning
50) The Might of Small Beginning
51) Understanding the Mysteries of Prophesy
52) Overcoming Dream Nightmares
53) Breaking the Shackles of the Curse of the Law
54) Understanding the Joy of Harvest
55) Wisdom for Signs & Wonders

56) Wisdom for Generational Impact
57) Wisdom for Marriage Stability
58) Understanding the Number of Your Days
59) Enforcing Your Kingdom Rights
60) Escaping the Traps of Immoralities
61) Escaping the Trap of Poverty
62) Accessing Biblical Prosperity
63) Accessing True Riches in Christ
64) Silencing the Voice of the Accuser
65) Overcoming the Forces of Oppositions
66) Quenching the Voice of the Avenger
67) Silencing Demonic Prediction & Projection
68) Silencing Your Mocker
69) Understanding the Power of the Holy Ghost
70) Understanding the Baptism of Power
71) The Mystery of the Blood of Jesus
72) Understanding the Mystery of Sanctification
73) Understanding the Power of Holiness
74) Understanding the Forces of Purity & Righteousness
75) Activating the Forces of Vengeance
76) Appreciating the Mystery of Restoration
77) Overcoming the Projection & Prediction of the Enemy
78) Engaging the Mystery of the Blood
79) Commanding the Power of the Speaking Faith
80) Uprooting the Forces Against Your Rising
81) Overcoming Mere Success Syndrome
82) Understanding Divine Sentence
83) Understanding the Mystery of Praise
84) Understanding the Author of Faith
85) The Mystery of the Finisher of Faith

MIRACLE OF GOD MINISTRIES

NIGERIA CRUSADE   2012

MIRACLE OF GOD MINISTRIES
NIGERIA CRUSADE 2012

MIRACLE OF GOD MINISTRIES

NIGERIA CRUSADE

2012

MIRACLE OF GOD MINISTRIES

NIGERIA CRUSADE

2012

www.ingramcontent.com/pod-product-compliance
Lightning Source LLC
Chambersburg PA
CBHW021449080526
44588CB00009B/766